PULLEYS
PULL THEIR WEIGHT

SIMPLE MACHINES *FOR KIDS*

Andi Diehn

Illustrated by Micah Rauch

EXPLORE THE BIOMES IN THIS PICTURE BOOK SCIENCE SET!

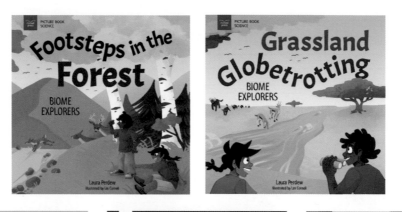

Check out more titles at www.nomadpress.net

Nomad Press

A division of Nomad Communications

10 9 8 7 6 5 4 3 2 1

This book was manufactured by CGB Printers,
North Mankato, Minnesota, United States
October 2023, Job #1066635

ISBN Softcover: 978-1-64741-090-2
ISBN Hardcover: 978-1-64741-087-2

Educational Consultant, Marla Conn

Questions regarding the ordering of this book should be addressed to
Nomad Press
PO Box 1036, Norwich, VT 05055
www.nomadpress.net

Printed in the United States.

When we have some heavy lifting to do—

A boulder on our banana,

A rhinoceros on our raspberries,

A pyramid on our pizza—

Our best bet?

Build a pulley!

A rope, a wheel, and
some tugging power
are all you need

To magnify your muscles,

Amplify your effort,

And lift more than you ever have before.

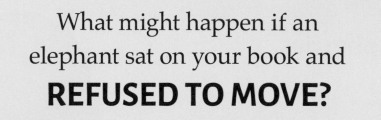

What might happen if an elephant sat on your book and **REFUSED TO MOVE?**

What can you do?

Even a baby elephant is

TOO HEAVY

for humans
to move!

You need help.
You need a
simple machine!

Simple machines
help us do work.

A **PULLEY** is a
simple machine.

A pulley is made of at
least one **wheel** and
a **rope or chain**.

**Other simple machines include
screws, levers, wedges, inclined
planes, and wheels and axles.**

Here's how a pulley works:

One end of the rope is attached to the **HEAVY OBJECT** you need to move— this object is called the **LOAD.**

Like the elephant!

Your rope is threaded around the wheel, which has a **GROOVE** so the rope doesn't SLIP OUT.

To work the pulley, someone **_PULLS_** at the loose end of the rope.

What happens?

UP GOES **THE ELEPHANT!**

A simple machine is a device that changes the direction or strength of a force.

Did you
suddenly get

VERY,

VERY

STRONG?   No—that's the **power of the pulley.**

A pulley gives you something called a **mechanical advantage.**

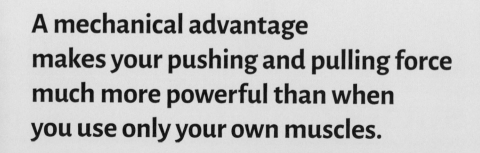

A mechanical advantage
makes your pushing and pulling force
much more powerful than when
you use only your own muscles.

Using just your own strength, you can *PUSH* and **PULL** on that elephant only so much before your muscles say, "NO! Too heavy! WE QUIT!"

But if you use a **pulley,** you can change the direction of that force.

Instead of trying to
lift the elephant,
you loop a rope
around the elephant
and pull down
on the other end
of the rope.

This kind of pulley
is called a
fixed pulley system.

**Pulling down to move a heavy
object is easier than lifting it.**

Another kind of pulley system is a **moveable pulley.**

Have you ever *zoooooomed* on a zip line?
That's a moveable pulley!

With a **moveable pulley,** both ends of the rope are attached to **different points**. The **load** is connected to the **pulley,** which moves **between the points.**

You can find moveable pulleys at construction sites, where large machines work to move very heavy materials.

A moveable pulley uses even LESS ENERGY to do MORE WORK.

Let's go back to your problem elephant.

What happens if the first pulley you made still isn't **strong enough** to lift it?

That's when it's time to use a **compound pulley.**

Two pulleys!

A **compound pulley** is a pulley with **more than one wheel**—one that is **fixed** and one that is **moveable**. The **more wheels** you add, the **more force** you have.

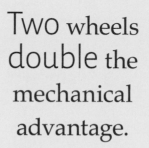

Two wheels **double** the mechanical advantage.

Three wheels **triple** the mechanical advantage.

Can you guess what **four wheels** do?

FIVE WHEELS?

YES!

Four wheels
quadruple and
FIVE wheels
QUINTUPLE the
amount of mechanical advantage
your pulley gives you.

And that elephant is GOING UP!

Pulleys are useful for many different types of work.

You can see pulleys in action
on your **window blinds**.

PULL on one string and the blinds go UP.

Do you have **exercise machines** in your home? Machines with weights have pulley systems so people can work their muscles in different ways.

You can find pulleys on **boats**, at **construction sites**, on **theater curtains**, and in many other places!

Humans have been
using pulleys for
thousands of years!

Legend says an ancient Greek thinker
named **Archimedes** was able to move the
largest ship in Greece ALL BY HIMSELF.

His secret?

A PULLEY!

23

People used pulley systems to help build the **Great Wall of China**.

The Great Wall of China was built more than 2,000 years ago as different Chinese emperors tried to defend their territories from invaders.

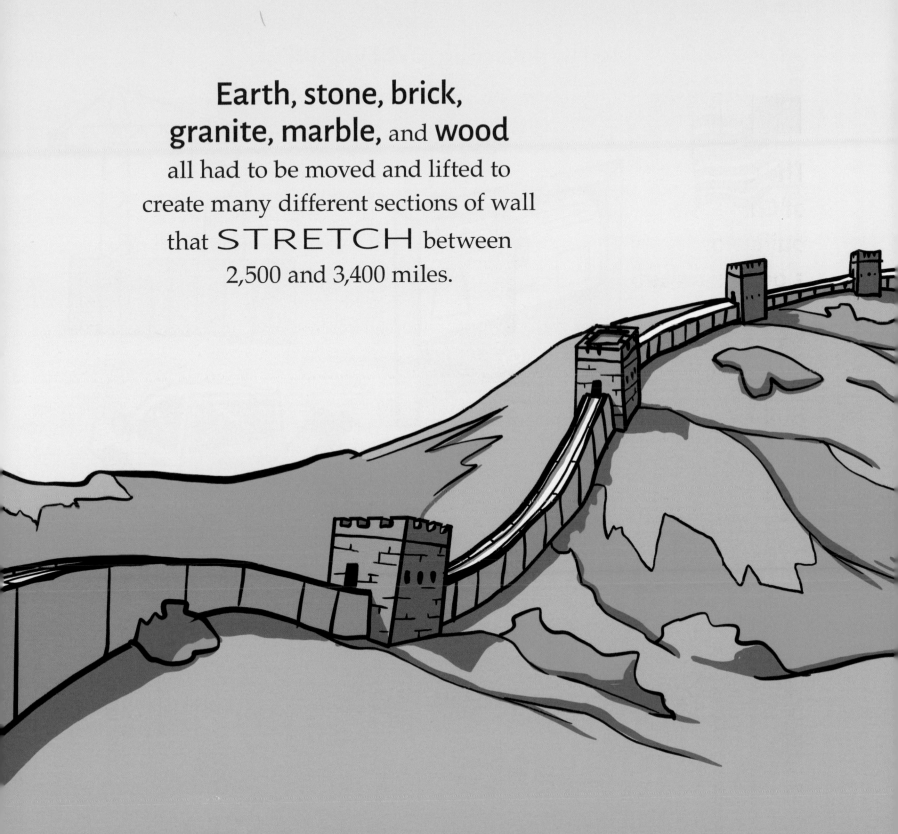

Earth, stone, brick,
granite, marble, and wood
all had to be moved and lifted to
create many different sections of wall
that STRETCH between
2,500 and 3,400 miles.

Today, pulleys are **everywhere!**

Look around your **house**, **school**, and **neighborhood**.
Where do you see pulleys?
What are they helping to lift?

And remember, whenever you need to
move an elephant, be sure to use a **PULLEY!**

Make a Pulley!

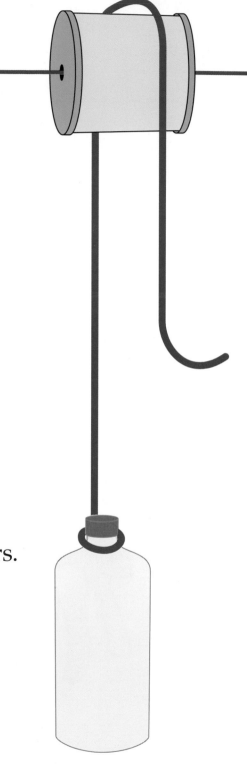

What You Need

one yogurt container and two lids - tape or glue - wooden skewer - string - bottle of water

What You Do

- Tape or glue the two lids onto each end of the yogurt container.

- Ask an adult to make a hole in each end of the container.

- Push the skewer through the holes so the container can turn around it easily. This is your pulley wheel!

- Balance the skewer on the backs of two chairs.

- Loop the string over your pulley wheel and tie one end to the water bottle.

Try It Out! Pull on the other end of the string. Can you lift the water bottle? Can you lift something heavier?

Glossary

compound pulley: a system of fixed and moveable pulleys that work together.

fixed pulley: a pulley system in which the pulley is fixed to a point and the rope is attached to the load or object.

force: a push or pull that changes an object's motion.

friction: a force that slows objects when they rub against each other.

inclined plane: a sloped surface that connects a lower level to a higher level.

lever: a bar that rests on a support and lifts or moves things.

load: an applied force or weight.

mechanical advantage: the amount a machine increases or changes a force to make a task easier.

moveable pulley: a pulley that moves together with the load.

pulley: a wheel with a grooved rim that a rope or chain is pulled through to help lift a load.

screw: an inclined plane wrapped around a central axis used to lift objects or hold things together.

simple machine: a device that changes the direction or strength of a force. The six simple machines are the inclined plane, lever, pulley, screw, wedge, and wheel and axle.

wedge: thick at one end and narrow at the other, a wedge is used for splitting, tightening, and securing objects.

wheel and axle: a wheel with a rod that turn together to lift and move loads.

work: the force applied to an object to move it across a distance.

Inclined Plane

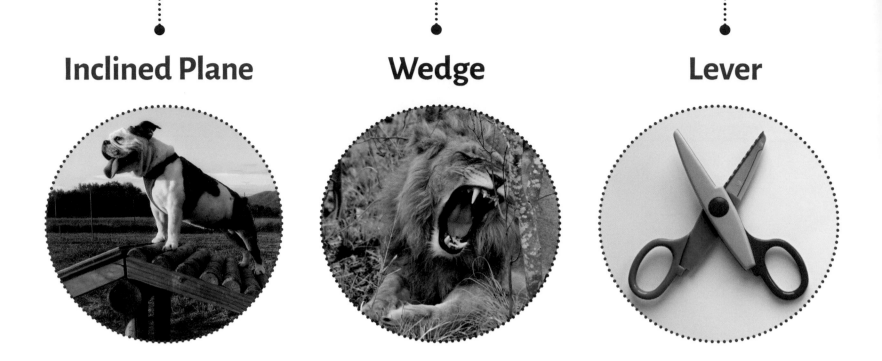

Wedge

Lever

SIMPLE MACHINES

Pulley

Screw

Wheel and Axle